HOW TO MAKE MONEY WITH ONLINE COURSES: TRANSFORM YOUR EXPERTISE INTO PROFITABLE LEARNING VENTURES

Introduction:

Welcome to "How to Make Money With Online Courses: Transform Your Expertise into Profitable Learning Ventures." In the digital era, online courses have emerged as a powerful means for individuals like you to share knowledge, teach valuable skills, and create a sustainable income stream. Whether you're an expert in a specific field, a passionate educator, or an entrepreneur with specialized knowledge, online courses offer a unique opportunity to monetize your expertise.

In this course, we will explore the strategies and tactics that will help you harness the potential of online courses to maximize your financial success.

From designing engaging course content to attracting a target audience and implementing effective monetization methods, we will cover every aspect of the process. By the end of this course, you will be equipped with the knowledge and tools to thrive in the competitive world of online course monetization.

Throughout this journey, we will delve into the art of creating captivating online courses that captivate learners, establish your authority, and generate substantial revenue. We will explore various monetization models, from selling courses directly to implementing membership subscriptions, leveraging affiliate marketing, or exploring partnerships and collaborations. With a focus on quality content, effective marketing, and strategic pricing, this course will empower you to turn your passion and expertise into a profitable learning venture.

Whether you're just starting out or have some experience in online course creation, this course is designed to meet you where you are and take your online course revenue to new heights. So, let's embark on this transformative journey together, uncovering the potential of online courses to generate income while making a positive impact on learners worldwide. Get ready to unlock the power of online courses and embark on a path to financial success. Let's get started!

What Are Online Courses

Online courses are educational programs or learning experiences delivered over the internet. They provide individuals with the opportunity to acquire knowledge, learn new skills, or enhance existing ones through a structured curriculum offered in a digital format.

Online courses can cover a wide range of subjects, including academic disciplines, professional skills, personal development, hobbies, and more. They are typically designed to be self-paced, allowing learners to access course materials and progress through the content at their own convenience.

Online courses often include a combination of multimedia elements such as video lectures, slideshows, readings, quizzes, assignments, discussion forums, and interactive activities. These components facilitate engagement, interaction, and knowledge retention.

Key features and benefits of online courses include:

Flexibility: Online courses offer flexibility in terms of scheduling and location. Learners can access course materials and participate in learning activities from anywhere with an internet connection, allowing them to study at their own pace and fit learning into their existing commitments.

Self-Paced Learning: Online courses are typically self-paced, allowing learners to progress through the material at their preferred speed. This flexibility caters to different learning styles and allows individuals to revisit or review content as needed.

Access to Expertise: Online courses often feature instructors who are subject matter experts in their fields. Learners can benefit from their knowledge and experience, receiving guidance, insights, and feedback throughout the course.

Interactive Learning: Online courses may incorporate interactive elements such as quizzes, assignments, discussion forums, or collaborative projects. These features facilitate active learning, engagement, and the application of knowledge in practical contexts.

Personalized Learning: Many online courses offer personalized learning experiences, allowing learners to choose specific modules or topics based on their interests or goals. Learners can focus on areas that are most relevant to them, maximizing the value they derive from the course.

Networking and Community: Online courses often provide opportunities for learners to connect with peers, share ideas, and engage in discussions through online forums or social platforms. This fosters a sense of community and enables collaborative learning experiences.

Accessibility: Online courses remove geographical barriers and make education accessible to a global audience. Individuals from different locations and backgrounds can access the same course content, eliminating the limitations of physical classrooms.

Online courses can be offered by educational institutions, universities, professional organizations, or independent instructors through dedicated learning platforms or learning management systems (LMS). Learners typically enroll in these courses by registering and paying a fee, although some online courses may be offered for free.

Overall, online courses provide a flexible and convenient way for individuals to acquire knowledge, develop skills, and pursue lifelong learning opportunities in a digital format.

How To Create Online Courses Putting Target Audience Into Consideration

Creating online courses with the target audience in mind is crucial for designing relevant, engaging, and effective learning experiences. Here are steps to consider when creating online courses that align with your target audience:

Define Your Target Audience: Clearly identify and understand your target audience. Consider their demographics, existing knowledge or skill level, goals, motivations, challenges, and preferred learning styles. This information will guide your course design and content development.

Set Clear Learning Objectives: Define specific learning objectives that align with your target audience's needs and expectations. Identify the key knowledge, skills, or outcomes you want learners to achieve by the end of the course. Clear objectives ensure focus and provide a sense of direction throughout the course creation process.

Conduct Audience Research: Conduct surveys, interviews, or market research to gather insights directly from your target audience. Ask about their learning preferences, pain points, and what they hope to gain from an online course. Use this information to tailor the course content, format, and delivery to meet their needs.

Structure the Course Content: Organize the course content in a logical and sequential manner. Break it down into modules or lessons, and ensure a smooth progression from basic to advanced concepts. Consider your audience's existing knowledge level and provide appropriate scaffolding or prerequisites if necessary.

Use Engaging and Multimedia Elements: Incorporate a variety of engaging multimedia elements such as video lectures, interactive quizzes, case studies, infographics, or real-world examples. Different learning styles and preferences should be taken into account to enhance learner engagement and comprehension.

Apply Active Learning Strategies: Encourage active learning by incorporating interactive activities, discussions, and hands-on exercises. These activities should relate to real-world scenarios or challenges your target audience may encounter. They help learners apply the knowledge and skills they acquire, enhancing their understanding and retention.

Provide Practical Examples and Applications: Illustrate concepts with practical examples, case studies, or real-life applications relevant to your target audience. Show how the knowledge or skills learned in the course can be applied in their specific contexts, making the content more relatable and valuable.

Use Clear and Conversational Language: Write course content using clear and concise language. Avoid jargon or technical terms unless necessary, and use a conversational tone to maintain engagement and accessibility. Break down complex concepts into digestible explanations to enhance understanding.

Offer Assessments and Feedback: Include assessments or quizzes throughout the course to help learners gauge their progress and reinforce their understanding. Provide feedback on assignments or assessments to guide learners and address any misconceptions or gaps in knowledge.

Incorporate Learner Support and Resources: Provide additional resources, references, or supplementary materials that cater to different learning preferences or levels. Offer support channels such as discussion forums, Q&A sessions, or email support to address learner questions or concerns.

Iterate and Seek Feedback: Continuously evaluate and improve your course based on learner feedback. Encourage participants to provide feedback on their learning experience and make necessary updates to enhance the course's effectiveness and relevance.

By keeping your target audience at the forefront of your course creation process, you can design online courses that meet their specific needs, engage them effectively, and provide a valuable learning experience. Regularly assess and refine your courses to ensure they remain relevant and aligned with evolving learner expectations.

How To Create Online Courses Putting Market Demands Into Consideration

Creating online courses that align with market demands is essential for ensuring that your courses meet the needs and preferences of your target audience. Here are steps to consider when creating online courses with market demands in mind:

Research the Market: Conduct market research to identify current trends, demands, and gaps in the market related to your course topic. Look for popular keywords, search volume, and competition. Explore existing online courses and analyze their offerings, pricing, and positioning to understand the market landscape.

Identify Marketable Topics: Select course topics that have significant demand in the market. Look for subjects that are in high demand, where there is a gap in quality courses, or where you have unique expertise or perspective to offer. Consider the relevance, applicability, and long-term value of the topic to ensure its marketability.

Analyze Competitors: Study competing online courses within your chosen topic area. Identify what they offer, their strengths, weaknesses, and areas where you can differentiate your course. Understand their pricing strategies, target audience, and the unique value propositions they provide. Use this information to position your course effectively in the market.

Define Unique Selling Points: Identify the unique selling points (USPs) that will set your course apart from competitors. This could be your expertise, teaching style, exclusive content, practical applications, interactive elements, or any other value-added features that differentiate your course. Clearly communicate these USPs in your course marketing materials.

Align Course Content with Market Needs: Ensure that the content of your course directly addresses the pain points, challenges, and aspirations of your target audience. Design modules, lessons, and activities that provide practical solutions, relevant case studies, or real-world applications. Make sure your course content reflects the current industry best practices and emerging trends.

Consider Course Format and Delivery: Assess the preferences and learning styles of your target audience and determine the most effective course format and delivery methods. Consider whether your audience prefers video-based instruction, interactive modules, downloadable resources, live webinars, or a combination of formats. Align your course structure and delivery to meet these preferences.

Stay Updated and Relevant: Continuously monitor market trends and developments in your field. Regularly update your course content to ensure it remains relevant and up-to-date. This demonstrates your commitment to providing the latest and most valuable information, enhancing the market appeal of your course.

Test and Validate: Before fully launching your course, consider offering a pilot version or beta version to a select group of participants. Collect feedback and testimonials from these participants to validate the market demand and effectiveness of your course. Make necessary adjustments based on their input before scaling up your course offering.

Develop a Strong Marketing Strategy: Once your course is created, develop a comprehensive marketing strategy to promote your course effectively. Utilize online marketing channels such as social media, email marketing, content marketing, search engine optimization (SEO), and paid advertising to reach your target audience. Highlight the market demand for your course in your marketing messages.

Gather and Utilize Customer Feedback: Encourage course participants to provide feedback and testimonials about their experience with your course. Collect and showcase positive feedback to build social proof and enhance the market perception of your course. Use customer feedback to make iterative improvements and cater to evolving market demands.

By considering market demands when creating online courses, you can ensure that your courses meet the needs of your target audience and have a higher chance of success in the competitive online learning market. Continuous monitoring of market trends and adapting your courses accordingly will help you stay ahead of the curve and deliver valuable content that resonates with your audience.

How To Create Online Courses Putting Your Passion And Expertise Into Consideration

Creating online courses that reflect your passion and expertise can lead to engaging, authentic, and impactful learning experiences for your audience. Here are steps to consider when creating online courses with your passion and expertise in mind:

Identify Your Passion and Expertise: Reflect on your areas of passion and expertise. Consider the subjects or topics that genuinely interest and excite you. Identify the areas where you have extensive knowledge, experience, or unique insights to offer. Choosing a topic aligned with your passion and expertise will help you stay motivated and deliver compelling content.

Define Learning Outcomes: Clearly define the learning outcomes you want your course participants to achieve. Based on your passion and expertise, identify the specific knowledge, skills, or transformations you want your audience to gain by completing the course. Focus on outcomes that align with your expertise and can provide tangible value to your learners.

Plan Course Structure and Content: Outline the structure and content of your course based on your passion and expertise. Break down the subject matter into modules or lessons that logically progress and build upon each other. Map out the key concepts, practical applications, examples, and activities you want to include. Ensure that the content reflects your unique perspective and insights.

Incorporate Practical Applications: Infuse your course with practical applications that highlight how the knowledge or skills you are sharing can be applied in real-life situations. Provide relevant case studies, examples, or exercises that allow participants to practice and apply what they learn. Practical applications help learners see the immediate relevance and value of the course content.

Use Engaging Teaching Methods: Leverage your passion and expertise to deliver the course content in engaging and dynamic ways. Incorporate storytelling, personal anecdotes, real-world examples, or visuals that bring the material to life. Share your enthusiasm and energy throughout the course to captivate and inspire your audience.

Create Interactive Learning Experiences: Design interactive learning experiences that encourage active participation and engagement. Incorporate quizzes, discussions, assignments, or group activities that allow participants to interact with the content and with each other. Foster a sense of community and collaboration to enhance the learning experience.

Provide Personalized Support: Offer personalized support to your course participants. This could include answering questions, providing feedback on assignments or projects, or offering one-on-one consultations or coaching sessions. Personalized support demonstrates your commitment to their success and enhances the learning journey.

Continuously Improve and Innovate: Stay curious and keep learning in your area of passion and expertise. Stay up to date with the latest developments, research, and industry trends. Continuously seek feedback from your participants and incorporate their input into course updates and improvements. Strive to innovate and offer new perspectives to keep your courses fresh and valuable.

Communicate Your Passion and Expertise: Clearly communicate your passion and expertise in your course materials and marketing efforts. Share your story, background, and qualifications to establish credibility and build trust with your audience. Let your enthusiasm and expertise shine through in your videos, presentations, and course materials.

Seek Collaboration and Feedback: Collaborate with others in your field or industry to gain different perspectives and insights. Seek feedback from peers, mentors, or beta testers to ensure your course effectively reflects your passion and expertise. Incorporate diverse perspectives to create a well-rounded and comprehensive learning experience.

By infusing your passion and expertise into your online courses, you can create unique and valuable learning experiences for your audience. Your genuine enthusiasm and deep knowledge will resonate with learners and inspire them to engage with the content, fostering a meaningful learning journey.

How To Establish A Clear And Compelling Learning Outcome In Your Online Courses

Establishing clear and compelling learning outcomes is essential for guiding your online course design and ensuring that your participants have a clear understanding of what they will achieve by the end of the course. Here are steps to establish clear and compelling learning outcomes in your online courses:

Identify the Core Concepts: Identify the key concepts, skills, or knowledge that you want your participants to gain from the course. Determine the essential elements that form the foundation of your course content. These core concepts will guide the development of your learning outcomes.

Use Action Verbs: Craft learning outcomes using specific and actionable verbs that describe the desired actions or behaviors participants will demonstrate after completing the course. Use verbs such as "analyze," "apply," "create," "evaluate," or "synthesize" to clearly communicate the level of cognitive engagement or skill mastery expected from participants.

Make Outcomes Measurable: Ensure that your learning outcomes are measurable and observable. This allows you and your participants to assess progress and achievement. Use verbs that can be measured, such as "design three marketing campaigns," "solve five complex equations," or "identify and discuss key theories." Measurable outcomes provide clarity and enable learners to gauge their progress.

Align Outcomes with Course Content: Ensure that each learning outcome directly relates to the course content and activities. The outcomes should reflect what participants will be able to do or understand as a result of engaging with the course materials and completing the assignments. Aligning outcomes with the content ensures relevance and coherence in the learning experience.

Consider Bloom's Taxonomy: Utilize Bloom's Taxonomy, a hierarchical framework for categorizing cognitive skills, to structure and scaffold your learning outcomes. Start with lower-level outcomes such as remembering or understanding, and progress to higher-level outcomes such as analyzing, evaluating, or creating. This ensures a balanced and progressive learning experience.

Prioritize Relevance and Applicability: Emphasize the relevance and applicability of the learning outcomes to the real world. Connect the outcomes to practical scenarios, problems, or contexts that participants are likely to encounter. Highlight how the skills or knowledge they gain can be applied in their personal or professional lives.

Communicate Benefits and Value: Clearly articulate the benefits and value that participants will derive from achieving the learning outcomes. Explain how the outcomes will help them overcome challenges, enhance their skills, achieve specific goals, or advance in their careers. Emphasize the practical value and potential impact on their lives.

Review and Refine: Regularly review and refine your learning outcomes based on participant feedback, industry changes, or emerging trends. Continuously assess whether the outcomes accurately reflect the course content and meet the needs of your target audience. Make necessary adjustments to ensure clarity, relevance, and alignment.

Communicate Learning Outcomes Effectively: Clearly communicate the learning outcomes to your participants at the beginning of the course. Include them in the course introduction, syllabus, or learning materials. Reiterate and reinforce the outcomes throughout the course to remind participants of what they are working towards.

Assess and Evaluate Outcomes: Design assessments or evaluations that align with the learning outcomes to measure participants' achievement and progress. Use formative and summative assessments to gauge their understanding, application, or mastery of the desired knowledge or skills. Assessments provide feedback and validate the attainment of the learning outcomes.

Establishing clear and compelling learning outcomes provides focus and direction to your online course design. It sets expectations for participants, guides your instructional decisions, and ensures that your course delivers tangible value and measurable results.

How To Create Engaging Course Material Organized Into Manageable Modules

To create engaging course material organized into manageable modules and include illustrations, follow these steps:

Determine Course Structure: Break down your course content into logical sections or modules based on the topics or subtopics you want to cover. Each module should focus on a specific theme or concept. Consider the flow and progression of the content, ensuring that modules build upon one another and create a coherent learning journey.

Set Learning Objectives for Each Module: Define clear learning objectives for each module. These objectives should outline what participants will achieve or learn by the end of the module. Learning objectives provide a sense of purpose and guide the development of module content.

Chunk Information: Break down the content within each module into smaller, manageable chunks. Avoid overwhelming participants with large blocks of text or lengthy videos. Instead, present information in bite-sized pieces that are easy to comprehend and retain. Use headings, subheadings, bullet points, and short paragraphs to enhance readability.

Incorporate Varied Content Formats: Use a mix of content formats to engage participants and cater to different learning styles. Include text-based content, videos, audio clips, infographics, interactive activities, quizzes, or downloadable resources. This variety keeps learners engaged and allows them to process information in different ways.

Utilize Visual Illustrations: Enhance the visual appeal of your course materials by incorporating illustrations, diagrams, charts, or images. Visual elements help to break up text and make the content more engaging and memorable. Use illustrations to simplify complex concepts, reinforce key points, or provide examples.

Use Storytelling Techniques: Weave storytelling elements into your course material to make it more relatable and engaging. Share personal anecdotes, case studies, or real-world examples that illustrate the practical application of the concepts being taught. Storytelling creates a connection with participants and enhances their understanding.

Provide Interactive Elements: Include interactive elements within your modules to foster engagement and active learning. Incorporate quizzes, interactive exercises, discussion forums, or group activities that encourage participants to apply what they have learned and interact with fellow learners. Interactive elements promote participation and reinforce learning.

Ensure Visual Consistency: Maintain visual consistency throughout your course material to create a cohesive and professional look. Use consistent color schemes, fonts, and formatting. Align your illustrations and visuals with the overall course design and branding. Consistency enhances the visual appeal and professionalism of your course.

Balance Content and Multimedia: Strike a balance between content and multimedia elements. Avoid overwhelming participants with excessive visuals or multimedia that distract from the core content. Ensure that illustrations and multimedia enhance the learning experience and serve a purpose in conveying information effectively.

Test and Iterate: Regularly test your course materials with a small group of participants or beta testers to gather feedback. Assess their engagement, comprehension, and overall learning experience. Based on their input, make necessary adjustments, improvements, or refinements to optimize the engagement and effectiveness of your course materials.

By organizing your course content into manageable modules and incorporating engaging illustrations, you create a visually appealing and immersive learning experience. Strive to deliver information in a way that is easy to digest, varied in format, and enriched with interactive elements. This approach keeps participants engaged, facilitates learning, and enhances their overall experience.

41 Ways To Make Money From Online Courses

There are several ways to make money from online courses. Here are some common strategies:

1. Sell Your Course: The most direct way to make money from online courses is to sell them. You can create a course and charge a one-time fee or a recurring subscription fee for access to the course content. Platforms like Teachable, Udemy, and Thinkific allow you to host and sell your courses easily.

2. Create a Membership Site: Instead of selling individual courses, you can create a membership site where participants pay a recurring fee to access a library of courses, exclusive content, or additional resources. This model provides ongoing revenue as long as members continue their subscriptions.

3. Offer Upsells and Add-ons: Enhance your course offerings by providing upsells or add-ons. These can include premium content, personalized coaching or support, downloadable resources, or access to a private community. Upsells and add-ons provide additional

value to participants and generate additional revenue for your course.

4. Provide Group Coaching or Consulting: Offer group coaching or consulting sessions as a premium service alongside your courses. Participants can pay for the opportunity to receive personalized guidance, feedback, or support from you. Group coaching or consulting can be offered as a package or as an add-on to the course.

5. Affiliate Marketing: Incorporate affiliate marketing into your courses by recommending relevant products or services to your participants. When participants make a purchase through your affiliate link, you earn a commission. Choose products or services that align with your course content and provide value to your participants.

6. Corporate Training or Licensing: Approach companies or organizations and offer your course as a corporate training program. Customize the content to meet their specific needs and offer it as a package deal. Alternatively, consider licensing your course to organizations or other course creators who want to offer it to their audience.

7. Create Bundled Packages: Package multiple courses together as a bundled offering. This provides value to participants who are interested in multiple courses and allows you to increase the overall price. You can offer a discounted rate for the bundle compared to purchasing the courses individually.

8. Collaborate with Other Experts: Collaborate with other experts or influencers in your industry to create joint courses or bundle your courses together. This allows you to tap into their audience and expand your reach. You can either split the revenue generated from the collaboration or agree on a revenue-sharing arrangement.

9. Licensing Content to Institutions or Organizations: If you have specialized knowledge or expertise, consider licensing your course content to educational institutions, corporations, or organizations. They can use your course as part of their training or professional development programs and pay you a licensing fee.

10. Create and Sell Course Materials: Repurpose your course content into other formats such as e-books, workbooks, or downloadable resources. These materials can be sold as standalone products to supplement your courses and provide additional value to your audience.

11. Remember that creating high-quality, valuable content is key to monetizing your online courses successfully. Continuously evaluate and improve your courses based on participant feedback, industry trends, and market demands to maximize their value and revenue potential.

12. Certification or Accreditation Programs: Offer certification or accreditation programs alongside your courses. Participants who successfully complete the program and meet the requirements receive a recognized certification or accreditation, which can justify a higher price point and attract individuals looking to enhance their credentials.

13. Affiliate Program for Your Course: Set up an affiliate program for your course, where others can sign up as affiliates and earn a commission for every sale they generate. Affiliates can promote your course through their networks, websites, or social media platforms, expanding your reach and potentially increasing sales.

14. Live Workshops or Webinars: Host live workshops or webinars as an upsell or add-on to your online courses. Participants can pay to attend these live sessions, where you provide additional insights, interactive activities, or Q&A sessions. Live events

provide a more personalized and interactive learning experience, often commanding higher prices.

15. Sponsorship and Brand Partnerships: Seek sponsorship or brand partnership opportunities where companies or brands can sponsor or collaborate with you on your course. This can involve product placements, sponsored content, or joint promotional efforts. The sponsor or brand provides financial support or resources in exchange for exposure to your audience.

16. Speaking Engagements and Workshops: Leverage your expertise and reputation gained from your online courses to secure speaking engagements or workshop opportunities. You can offer keynote speeches, training sessions, or workshops at conferences, industry events, or corporate training programs. Speaking engagements can generate additional income and boost your course sales.

17. Licensing or Selling Course Content to Other Instructors: If you have created a successful online course, you can consider licensing or selling the rights to your course content to other instructors or course creators. They can use your content as part of their own courses, paying you a licensing fee or a percentage of the revenue generated.

18. Continuity Programs or Membership Subscriptions: Offer continuity programs or membership subscriptions where participants pay a recurring fee to access ongoing updates, new content, or exclusive resources related to your course. This provides a steady stream of revenue and fosters a sense of community among your audience.

19. Sponsored Content or Sponsored Guest Experts: Incorporate sponsored content or feature sponsored guest experts within your course. This involves partnering with relevant brands or experts who can provide value to your participants. The sponsors pay for the exposure and promotional opportunities within your course.

20. Create an Online Learning Platform: If you have a successful online course and a portfolio of courses, consider creating your own online learning platform. You can host and sell courses from multiple instructors, earning revenue from course sales and potentially taking a percentage of revenue generated by other instructors.

21. Offer Consulting or Coaching Services: Leverage your expertise and knowledge gained from your online course to offer consulting or coaching services. Participants who require more personalized guidance

or support can pay for one-on-one consulting sessions, coaching calls, or personalized feedback on their progress.

Remember, finding the right monetization strategies for your online courses may require experimentation and adaptation based on your audience, niche, and industry. Continuously assess the effectiveness of your strategies, track metrics, and adjust your approach to optimize revenue generation while maintaining the quality and value of your courses.

22. Corporate Training Programs: Partner with businesses or organizations to offer customized training programs based on your expertise. Tailor your course content to their specific needs and deliver it as a corporate training program. Corporate clients often pay higher fees for specialized training that aligns with their goals and objectives.

23. Group Licenses: Offer group licenses or bulk purchases of your course to organizations, schools, or institutions. This allows them to provide access to your course to multiple employees, students, or members at a discounted rate. Group licenses can be a cost-effective solution for organizations looking to offer training to a large number of individuals.

24. Affiliate Joint Ventures: Collaborate with other course creators or experts in complementary fields to create joint venture affiliate partnerships. Promote each other's courses to your respective audiences and earn a commission on sales generated through your affiliate links. This can expand your reach and generate additional revenue.

25. Premium Content or Upsells: Create premium content or upsells within your course that participants can purchase for an additional fee. This can include advanced modules, bonus resources, exclusive interviews, or extended access to the course materials. Premium content and upsells offer additional value to participants while generating extra income.

26. Sponsorship or Brand Collaborations: Partner with relevant brands or companies to collaborate on sponsored content or create co-branded courses. Brands can provide financial support, resources, or access to their audience in exchange for visibility and promotion within your course. Collaborations can be mutually beneficial and provide an additional revenue stream.

27. Affiliate Marketplaces: List your course on affiliate marketplaces or course directories where affiliates can discover and promote your course. Platforms like

ClickBank, ShareASale, or CJ Affiliate allow you to reach a wider network of affiliates who can drive traffic and sales to your course.

28. Continual Updates and Membership Renewals: Offer ongoing updates and new content to participants who have completed your course. Provide them with the option to renew their membership or access to the updated content for a recurring fee. Continual updates keep your course relevant and encourage participants to stay engaged and renew their membership.

29. Exclusive Partnerships with Influencers: Collaborate with influencers or thought leaders in your industry to offer exclusive partnerships. These influencers can promote your course to their audience through sponsored content, joint webinars, or dedicated promotions. This can significantly increase your course visibility and generate more sales.

30. Reseller or Licensing Programs: Develop reseller or licensing programs where other individuals or organizations can resell or offer your course under their own brand. They can market and sell your course to their audience, paying you a percentage of the revenue generated. Reseller or licensing programs can help expand your course's reach and generate passive income.

31. Cross-Promotion with Complementary Products or Services: Partner with individuals or businesses offering complementary products or services to cross-promote each other. For example, if you teach a course on photography, you can collaborate with a camera equipment supplier and offer special discounts to your participants. This mutually beneficial arrangement can generate additional revenue for both parties.

Remember, it's important to choose monetization strategies that align with your course, target audience, and goals. Continuously assess the effectiveness of your strategies, track key metrics, and adjust your approach to maximize revenue generation while delivering value to your participants.

32. Affiliate Launches: When launching a new course, partner with affiliates or influencers who can promote your course to their audience in exchange for a commission on sales. This leverages their reach and credibility to generate more course sales.

33. Create a Sales Funnel: Develop a sales funnel that guides potential customers from awareness to purchasing your course. This can include offering a free lead magnet or mini-course to capture email addresses, nurturing leads with valuable content, and

then promoting your paid course to interested subscribers.

34. Offer a Tiered Pricing Structure: Provide different pricing options for your course to cater to various budgets and customer segments. Offer a basic package at a lower price point and premium packages with additional features or personalized support at higher price points.

35. Continual Marketing and Promotion: Consistently market and promote your course through various channels, such as social media, email marketing, content marketing, guest blogging, podcast appearances, or webinars. Keep your course in front of your target audience and consistently communicate its value.

36. Create Bundled or Package Deals: Bundle multiple courses together or offer package deals that include additional resources or bonuses. This can incentivize customers to purchase multiple courses or upgrade to a higher-priced package, increasing your overall revenue.

37.Create an Affiliate Program for Your Course: Establish an affiliate program specifically for your course where others can sign up as affiliates and earn a commission for every sale they refer. Provide affiliates with marketing materials, promotional codes, and resources to support their promotional efforts.

38. Provide Continuing Education or Recurring Subscriptions: Offer ongoing education or membership programs where participants pay a recurring fee to access new course content, updates, live Q&A sessions, or community support. This provides a steady stream of revenue and encourages long-term engagement.

39. Develop Corporate Partnerships: Collaborate with companies or organizations to offer your course as part of their employee training or professional development programs. Work with HR departments or training managers to customize the course to meet their specific needs and negotiate corporate licensing or bulk purchases.

40. Offer Group or Team Discounts: Provide discounts or special pricing for groups or teams who enroll in your course together. This encourages team members or colleagues to sign up as a group, boosting sales volume and fostering a collaborative learning environment.

41. Create Limited-Time Offers and Flash Sales: Generate urgency and scarcity by offering limited-

time discounts, flash sales, or early bird pricing. This can motivate potential customers to take immediate action and make a purchase before the offer expires.

Remember to continuously assess and refine your monetization strategies based on customer feedback, market trends, and the evolving needs of your target audience. Experiment with different approaches and iterate as you gather data and insights to optimize your revenue generation from online courses.

Conclusion:

Congratulations! You have reached the end of "How to Money With Online Courses: Transform Your Expertise into Profitable Learning Ventures." Throughout this course, we have explored the strategies, techniques, and best practices that can help you monetize your expertise and create a thriving online course business.

We began by understanding the importance of designing engaging and valuable course content that resonates with your target audience. By leveraging your expertise and passion, you can create courses that captivate learners, provide them with tangible value, and establish your authority in your field.

We explored various methods of monetizing online courses, from selling them directly to implementing membership subscriptions, utilizing affiliate marketing, or seeking partnerships and collaborations. By adopting a strategic approach to pricing, marketing, and monetization models, you can generate substantial revenue while creating a sustainable income stream.

Additionally, we delved into effective marketing and promotion techniques to attract your ideal learners and grow your audience. By leveraging digital marketing channels, social media platforms, and email marketing, you can increase course enrollments and reach a wider audience who can benefit from your knowledge and expertise.

Remember that creating and monetizing online courses is an ongoing journey. Continuously seek feedback from your learners, stay updated on industry trends, and refine your course offerings to meet the evolving needs of your audience. By consistently delivering value and adapting to market demands, you can position yourself for long-term success in the online course industry.

As you apply the insights and strategies gained from this course, remember that financial success with online courses is within your reach. Embrace your expertise, unleash your creativity, and let your passion shine through your course content. Your dedication, coupled with the strategies learned, will empower you to transform your expertise into profitable learning ventures.

Thank you for joining us on this transformative learning journey. We wish you every success as you embark on your path to monetizing online courses and making a meaningful impact on learners worldwide. Get ready to create, inspire, and reap the financial rewards of your expertise. Best of luck in your online course monetization endeavors!

www.ingramcontent.com/pod-product-compliance
Lightning Source LLC
Chambersburg PA
CBHW072224290526
45794CB00007B/2873